A

DEBUT COLLECTION

FROM

LONELY PENGUIN
poetry

I was a broken mess of a man
struggling with my mental health.
So I picked up a pen;

and chose to write my way out of hell.
These pages are from my soul.
I had nothing but words to save me.
This is for anyone and everyone,
going through the same.
You are not alone.

For there is always hope
as long as we have words
to connect us.

To my wife and our two darling boys-
for never giving up on me

and for saving me in ways
that words cannot express.

The Lonely Penguin

First Printing, 2021

Printing information on last page.

ISBN-13: 9781989795064 (sc)

ISBN-13: 9781989795071 (eb)

Illustration: Simon Colinson

Book & Brand Design: Dot Ink Creative

THE
LONELY
PENGUIN

A POETRY COLLECTION

TABLE OF CONTENTS

I

This here, right at this moment,

could very well be the love

that changes it all.

Ordinary has a new meaning.

Nothing will ever be the same again.

You have redefined it all.

And that was the beauty of you.

You saw the holes, this hollow shell

and chose to fill it with love.

Not just any love.

The type that makes people forget

why they ache,

the type that fills the voids and cracks

and inspires them to live again.

You're the pressed flower between pages;

the faded handwritten love note,

the pocket watch that's lost its tick,

you are are timeless to me

and you always will be.

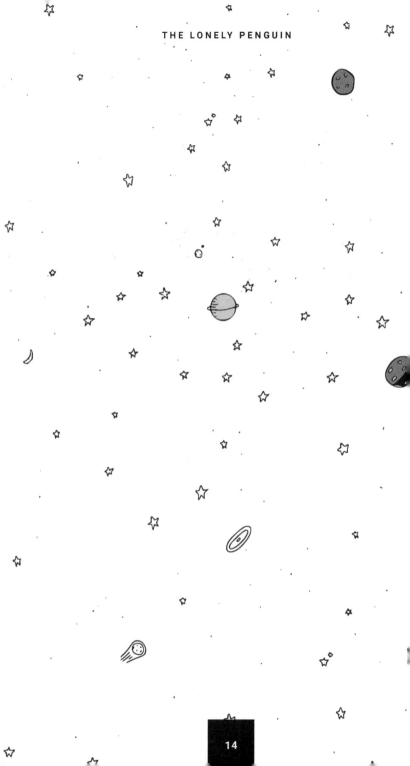

'I love you' just isn't enough.

I need you to know,

you're my first and last thought.

My light in the dark

and my universe full

of endless possibilities.

Dearest ghost,

I know you are waiting.

I know you are here.

I know you love me.

I know my dear.

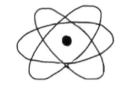

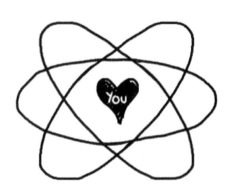

We are made of atoms
consisting almost entirely of empty space.

Yet amongst all of this emptiness,
my soul is full of nothing but love for you.

She is clumsy,

ditzy, wild and free.

But my word,

the care she took

with my heart.

I am not the same person
you met many years ago,
and neither are you.

But no matter how much time
or circumstance may change us,
we will always share the belief
that the me and you of yesterday
have never really left us.

And as long as we remember that,
our love will last forever.

Eyes as blue

as the ocean waves,

and here I am,

all lost at sea.

SIMON COLINSON

Let the stars rain down on us
as we kiss under a canopy of light.
And let the waves wash over us
as we drown in the tides of love.

Until the last star in the night sky
emits its last ray of light...
Until the last photon diminishes into the
everlasting darkness...

Know that I will forever love you
and I will go on loving you
in every other place, we both may be.

Fire will burn,

flowers will bloom.

And us:

forever, we'll be.

And what if love
is the coming together
of two lost souls-
torn-edged humans
looking for eternity?

If beautiful were a colour,
not even the finest artist
could recreate your palette.

You're a masterpiece
and a rare one at that.

As vast as the ocean is,

love extends beyond the eye.

My winter heart,

my mind like night...

I pray for those summer days,

yet you taught me love

comes in many forms...

my moon in my darkest phase.

When the winds no longer catch

your worn and weathered sails,

I will be there,

drifting with you

into forever.

Some are in love with war,

some are at war with love.

And me;

I don't want any of it.

I just want a love that's raw.

It doesn't matter

if I am lost,

as long as I

have you.

I think about a world
where things could have been
so much better
and it scares me to think:
What if this world is full of flaws
so you can be my better place.

Nature reminds me of
the rare purity in beginnings.
The solemn stillness of snow.

Raindrops bouncing
on the leaves around me.
The winter moon and its glow.

Nature reminds me of
the rare purity in beginnings.
A reminder of me and you.

And how we started
that winter's day.
A love so pure and true.

It took millennia to emerge:

It had seen hell and travelled across that dark void.

Its final resting place beautifully interrupted

by your perfect form.

You did it justice:

what a journey,

little photon.

There you are,

minding your own business,

in your own little world,

unknowingly breaking hearts.

You love like the sun greets the horizon,

You guide me like the stars on a dark night.

You kiss like the colours of a sunset.

You are my all,

my darkness,

my light.

I would leave this Earth in a Rocket Ship

and fly across the heavens,

if it meant I could hold you

one last time.

We have watched the stars together

so many times.

It's impossible to look up

and not think of you.

SIMON COLLINSON

PART I

This is a love note,
and this is for you.
You have unknowingly
carried me through
so much.
You have healed
deep sighs and dried
tears before they
could fall.
Your tiny frame has
held more weight than
my shoulders could ever carry.

PART II

Your smile will forever
and always be my symbol
of how the world should
conduct itself.
You don't even realise
all of the things that
you do.
You are unintentionally
and quite remarkably
beautiful.
This is a love note,
and this is
for you.

II

HEART
BREAK

I am trying to let go
one last "maybe" at a time.

That's the fucked up thing about love:

sometimes they'll hurt you

and all you want to do

is understand why.

I came back to the place where we first met,

maybe you will too...

Someday.

This is not a love letter,

this is goodbye.

A farewell to you.

My dreams came true

when you took my hand.

And so did all of my fears

when you decided to let go.

So allow me this simple request,

for the only fight I have left

is for me.

This is not a love letter.

This is goodbye.

Nothing much has changed since you left.

The place is a little untidy,

and I haven't slept the same.

But my heart still beats

the syllables of your name.

Don't be fooled by the light.

Sometimes its source

will lead you back to the flame.

What a curse it is

to have wings and not fly...

to be in love and not show it.

We fall in love,

but sometimes

we fall, in love.

Thinking of the future will kill you;
thinking of the past will torture.
The present is all you have.

PART I

I look for your reflection

in the windows of parked cars.

I hold my breath at 3 a.m.

with the hope of hearing yours.

I drink coffee just the way you liked it

so I can taste something familiar.

I long for the spring

and your sweet smell of blossom.

PART II

Every sense of you

has been taken away from me,

yet you will forever live

inside this hollow shell

I call home.

I can't let you go.

Not yet.

PART I

I've wandered our home, sat in my chair,
please acknowledge me.
I am so damn lost, I will try to explain
maybe I should leave you be.
You cry daily over my photo,
while I'm right here across the room.
I don't understand why you can't see me
but I know I am not in a tomb.
I'm beginning to think I'm just a ghost,
I can't even haunt your dreams.
I want to hold your hand again,
I wish you'd hear my screams.

PART II

So maybe I did pass but only to you
or maybe I am in denial.
I've visited the places we'll remember forever
and I see you walking down the aisle.
I followed you today for the first time in years;
you were crying in a cemetery
and then I knew why I couldn't move on,
on the tombstone was a picture of me.

You cannot know love
until you cry
over what you thought
love to be.

If I don't tell a soul,

the pain isn't real.

It doesn't exist.

-the lies we tell ourselves.

You broke me into a thousand tiny shards
then complained how much you bled
when you tried to walk all over me again.

Heed your gut.

Even hearts lie.

I wave goodbye with a brave smile
and through teary eyes I watch you go.
I hear echoes of all that we could have been
whispering in the wind.
I hear the leaves hush our song
and the swoosh of distant cars
begging you to turn around
and stay.

Even when the end is nigh,

I will always be here,

by your side.

I am only half here.

The other half still roams

the memories of a life

that will never be.

Please.

Come home.

I want to live again.

We wake
each morning
to no birdsong.
Maybe
they will sing
for us
tomorrow?

I am detached from the reality

that love never dies.

You see it does:

love dies in the most beautiful of ways

and the embers that remain

birth beautiful

new beginnings.

And when all is said and done.

The one you gave it all to

will be the one to break you.

And the one you owe it all to

is still a stranger.

Life can throw you in so many different directions,

and you feel left out in the wilderness.

Parts of life were never supposed to stay,

and others are now a permanent piece of you.

So if you ever feel like you've lost sight of the road-

Try to remember, even if it doesn't make sense just yet,

this is the path you were destined to follow.

We are neither kings nor Queens

Just humans,
with the same quest for happiness.

As the final leaf falls from the tree
it may look like this is the end.
As a feather drops, dancing on a breeze
it may feel like all hope is lost.
In time you'll see that for life to go on
we lose parts of ourselves
to feed wonderful new beginnings.

This sadness washes over me

like a never-ending tide.

I had drifted far out to sea.

Hope was all I had remaining

and there you were

lost amongst the waves like me.

We sailed on a breeze,

we caught the current...

We were no longer afraid and alone

as we sailed beyond the sunset

to a new day,

to a new place,

to a new home.

I hold onto the hope

that one day

we will be together again.

Like a feather in an open palm

waiting for a breeze to take us.

In time we will fly again.

I can't help but be a little scared

by your kind, beautiful heart

and the way you make

my voice shake.

There is dark in the stars,

there is light in us all.

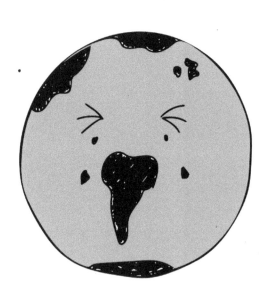

Weighed down
with the debt of owing
the world a smile
when I can't even
afford my own.

We are all but dormant flowers

waiting for our perfect sun

to bring us to life.

SIMON COLINSON

PART I

When I am no more and leave this plain,
I'll still be here with you,
for whenever you look to the sky for strength,
I will always guide you through.
When you wake and hear the first birdsong,
or see crystal drops of snow,
the movement of leaves in the trees above,
I am in those winds that blow.

PART II

When you hear the waves crash on the shore,

Or see the mist roll in,

I am in the thunder that shakes your soul,

I am present in everything.

You are not alone do not be afraid,

For it's only for a while,

We will meet again someday I promise,

But first, live long and smile.

If today hasn't quite gone to plan
and the sun didn't clear the cloud,
tomorrow you'll try again
and for that you should be proud.

I never knew I consisted

of this many parts.

This vessel full of memories,

hopes and doubts,

dreams and nightmares.

I discovered a piece of me

in every shard and every slither.

I found myself in the shattering of me.

PART I

What is poetry?

It is the rustling of leaves
in the trees above.
The cry of a newborn,
an unbinding love.
A songbird's chorus,
a morning dew.
The carrier of hope
to guide us through.

PART II

It's the crashing of waves
on a deserted shore.
cold winter mornings
and so much more.
It's the ache of a soul
dying to be freed.
Expressed with words
in a time of need.

What if we exist out there,

in a different realm?

Or a different time?

Through all the mistakes

I have made right here,

somewhere out there

you're mine.

Little Bird.

I promise you will fly again.

Please.

Don't fly home.

There is a world out there.

You belong in the clouds.

Not a cage.

To the world's
smallest superhero:

you save me
every day.

IV

RESIL
IENCE

I have put pen to paper a million times

and it was always seemingly you.

Today will be the start of a million and one reasons

why I will be somebody new.

Some days
you won't feel
good enough
for this world.
And on those days,
smile anyways.
Because you are
more than enough.

This future of mine

that you hold so delicately

in your hands...

You don't realise

how breakable I am,

but maybe I don't realise

how careful you are.

Fresh new beginnings are birthed

in these very depths.

Better days are coming,

you just don't know it yet.

Only on my down days

do I search for you

and the familiar.

And even then

I find the strength

within myself to pull away

and realise that our time has gone.

We are no more,

we are past tense

and my future now lies

in everything unfamiliar.

Maybe you'll never truly find someone

who loves you the way you love them.

But then again,

maybe they think the same.

124

Close your eyes, smell the air,

and taste the moment.

Fold the corner of this day.

Your book will have

many pitfalls and heartbreaks.

And when you need to find

the strength to carry on,

this will be the page you turn to.

During hard times you'll wish

for superhuman powers.

To fly away, to disappear,

to go back in time to a happier place.

Yet you fail to realise

that simply carrying on

is superhuman in itself.

I sometimes feel

I owe the world a sorry,

my head is so full of noise.

I need you to know

I'm trying my best.

Like a spring in a twisted poise.

These thoughts they haunt me

like a ghost

I wish would go away.

So I am sorry dear world

if I cant afford

one of your fake smiles today.

The light is yours to keep forever,

so take it if you will,

but first a little walk in darkness,

afraid is part of the thrill.

All I ask is that you
love yourself a little today,
and tomorrow I'll ask the same;
only a little more.
And bit by bit.
A year from now
you'll be saying the same
to others.

To finally reach indifference

and feel the calm to a hurt

that once plagued your life

is as good as any gift,

and a true sign that you

are on the right path to healing.

PART I

I'm a man made of stitches,
I'm falling apart at the seams.
I've cried in the shower,
showered my pillow in screams.

✳

So I smile at the world,
while they think I'm okay.
But little do they know,
I wish it would end today.

✳

So I wrote what I felt,
It still didn't make sense.
Pages of nothing,
every word more intense.

PART II

I shared some of these thoughts,
with people I've never met.
I'm not fighting this alone,
dear strangers of the net.

*

And slowly these stitches,
are knitting back together.
Thanks to this community,
I will treasure you forever.

ABOUT
SIMON

LONELY PENGUIN
poetry

Simon Colinson is an English poet and author who specializes in bridging the gap between heart and pen. His following grew almost overnight, leading him to pursue bringing his words to a physical form.

Simon uses his poetry as a tool to process emotions, celebrate successes, and connect with those who may be able to relate.

FIND SIMON ONLINE

Facebook.com/LonelyPenguinPoetry

Instagram.com/Lonely.Penguin

Tiktok.com/@LonelyPenguinPoetry

LonelyPenguin.com

It is Dot Ink's distinctive privilege to bring Simon's work to a physical medium.

We specialize in working with small businesses and creators to build lasting brands with undeniable impact.

WORK WITH US

Facebook.com/DotInkCreative

Instagram.com/DotInkCreate

THE
REVIEWS

"

In his collection, Simon was able to capture what I believe is the essence of what we are all searching for in this world: the undying hope of a brighter tomorrow. Within these words, there is one thing that you will surely find: a home.

A cozy shelter for the dark nights and a sweet companion for the good days. A promise that wondrous things happen and that we should never stop chasing them.

A book for anyone that wants to know or wants to remember what love truly is.

- F.E. MARIE

IG: @F.E.MARIE

"

A beautifully written and illustrated collection of moving poetry from one of my favorite writers. I just love the format and the imagery. It will take you on a magical journey through love, heartbreak, hope, and resilience. Something for every occasion, a book I will keep turning to.

– MATT SPENSER

IG: @MATTSPENSER

"

Simon opens doors for those who never
thought that they, too, could write poetry.
His journey takes you from the depths of
heartache into the bright beyond. It will
lead you to find the hope to persevere.
If you've ever wondered, "Does anybody
understand?" You'll find home here.

- BETH HUSTON

IG: @DOTINKCREATE

THANK
YOU

FOR
READING

WANT MORE
FROM SIMON?

USE YOUR PHONE TO
SCAN THE QR CODE.

Lightning Source UK Ltd.
Milton Keynes UK
UKHW050644230222
399109UK00006B/136